By Robert B. Pickering

Prepared under the direction of Robert Hillerich, Ph.D.

Library of Congress Cataloging in Publication Data
Pickering, Robert B.

I can be an archaeologist.

Includes index.
Summary: Describes, in simple text and illustrations, archaeology and the work of an archaeologist.
1. Archaeologists—Juvenile literature.
2. Archaeology—Juvenile literature. [1. Archaeologists.
2. Archaeology. 3. Occupations] I. Title.
CC107.P53 1987 930.1 87-14683
ISBN 0-516-01909-0

Childrens Press®, Chicago

Printed in the United States of America.
6 7 8 9 10 R 96 95

# PICTURE DICTIONARY

archaeologist

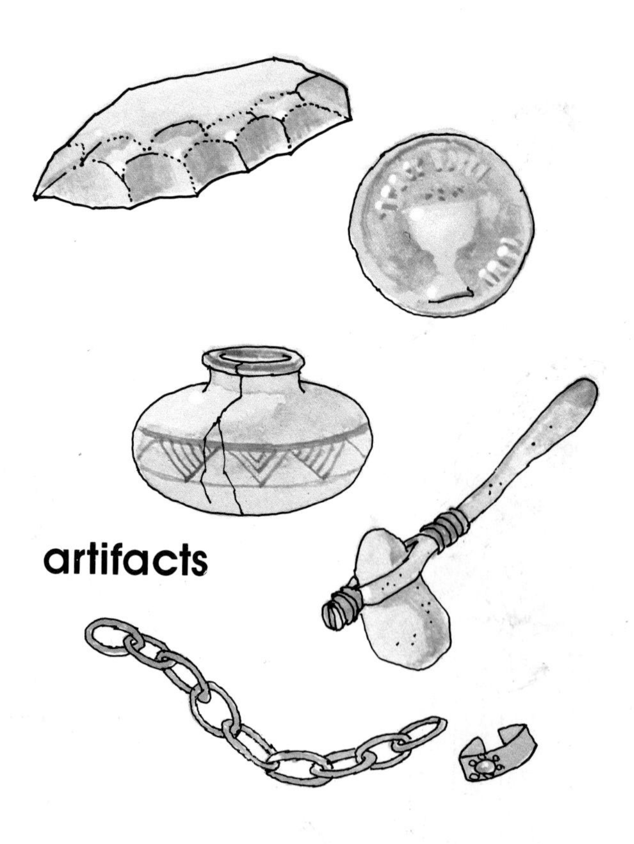

artifacts

archaeological site

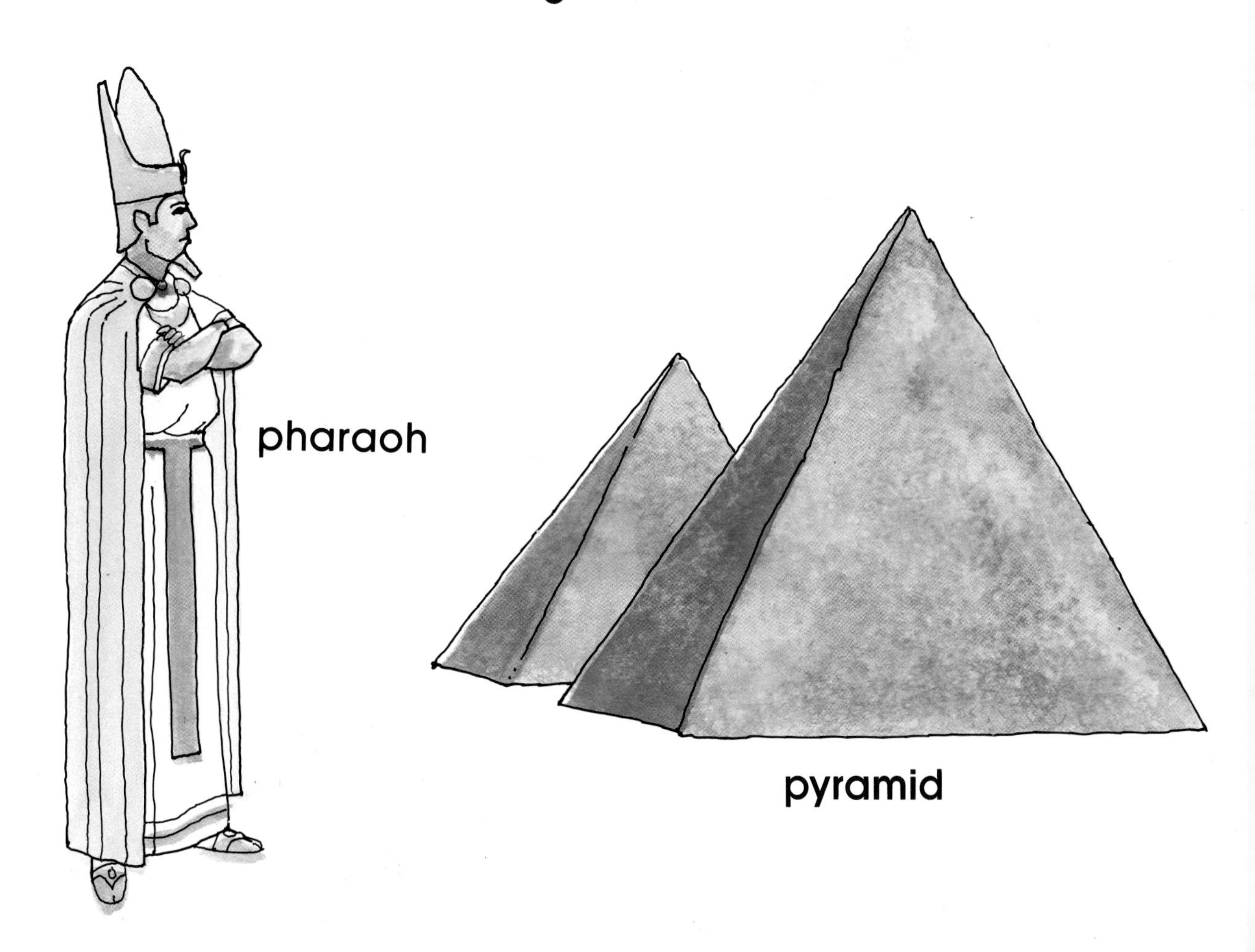

pharaoh

pyramid

Have you ever found something and asked yourself, "Who did this belong to?" You might have asked, "What is it?" "How is it used?" If so, you were thinking like an archaeologist.

An archaeologist is a scientist who studies how people lived hundreds and even thousands of years ago. Archaeologists

**archaeologist**

Opposite page: Archaeologists dig at a fifth century Saxon cemetery called Spong Hill.

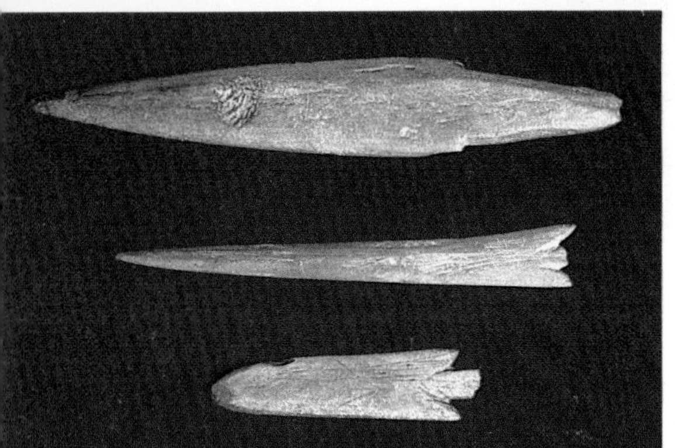

Tools, such as the milling stones (top left) from South Africa, the spear points (left) from North America, and the storage jars (above) from ancient Greece, tell archaeologists how ancient people lived.

learn about the past by asking questions. They look for the tools, jewelry, and houses that ancient people made. Archaeologists study these objects. They learn about the places and the people who lived there.

How do archaeologists learn about the people who lived and worked thousands of years ago? Archaeologists learn to "read" the objects they find just like you are reading this book. Any object made by humans is called an artifact. The book that you are reading and the clothes you are wearing are artifacts of modern

artifacts

people. Each artifact can tell a story if you know how to read it.

Artifacts are clues from the past. Like detectives who find clues, read them, and solve a case, archaeologists solve the mystery of what happened long ago.

Here is an artifact that you can read. Look at the picture of this penny. How many things can you tell

For more information about this penny see pages 28 and 29.

about the people who made it? Here are some hints:

1. When was it made?

2. From what material is it made?

3. What language did the people speak?

After you have made your list, compare it to the list of clues on pages 28 and 29.

You can "read" the penny because it is familiar. Its numbers and letters are the same ones that you use. The person on the penny is someone you have read about. If there is something about the penny that you don't understand, you can ask someone. You

Coin (left) pictures Alexander the Great, who ruled the kingdom of Macedonia from 336-323 B.C. The coin (above) pictures Tiberius Caesar, who ruled the Roman Empire from 14-37 A.D.

can find out more from books in the library.

Some ancient artifacts can be read easily because we still use similar things today. Compare the two coins shown above. The

Archaeologists must label everything they find.

country for each is different. However, many things about the coins are similar. How are the coins alike? How are they different?

Archaeologists often find artifacts that look very different from objects we make and use today.

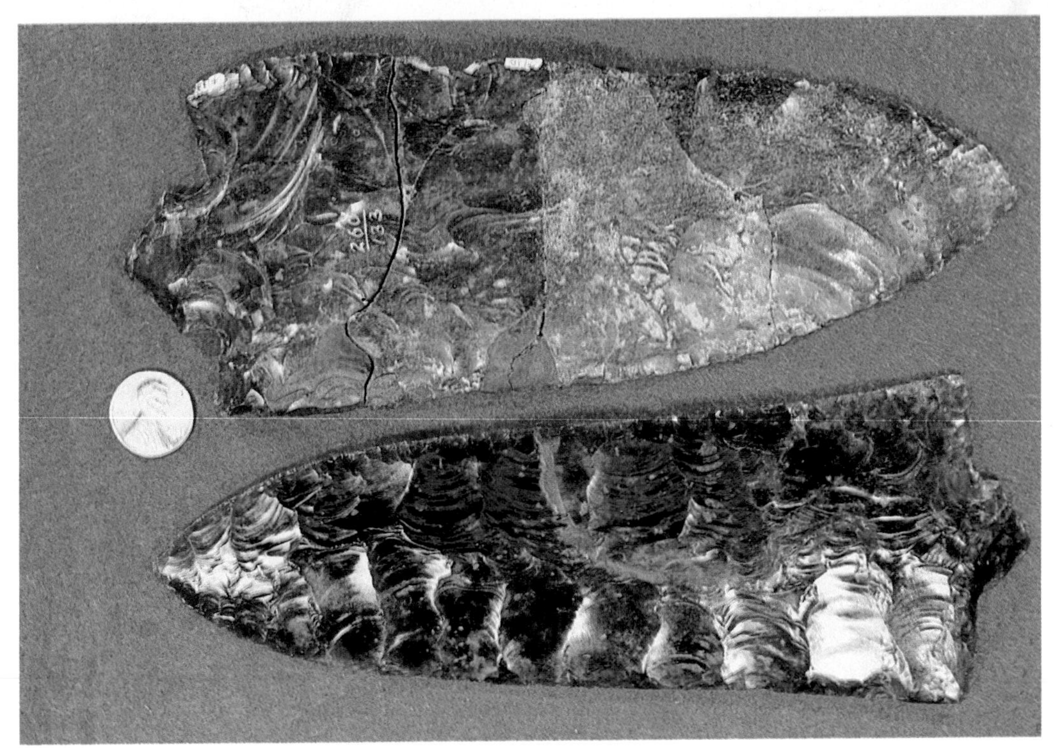

The penny clearly shows the size of the two blades found in Mound City, Ohio.

Here is a stone tool with a sharp edge. We might try to guess what the artifact is, but we can't know for certain without learning more about the tool and where it was found.

If you found this artifact with buffalo bones and

ashes from a fire, you might think it had something to do with preparing food. In fact, it is a knife made of stone. It was used thousands of years ago to cut up meat.

Archaeologists discover artifacts at archaeological sites. An archaeological site is a place where ancient people lived,

Archaeologists dig out a section of Hadrian's Wall in Great Britian

worked, or left things they made. By carefully studying the artifacts and the site, archaeologists can tell what people did there.

An archaeological site might once have been a

The castle (top left), the observatory (top right), the plumed serpent (bottom left) at the Temple of the Warriors (bottom right) stand at Chichen Itza as examples of an ancient civilization.

great city where thousands of people lived. Chichen Itza in southern Mexico had many temples and palaces. It was built over a thousand years ago.

The pyramids at Giza were built without using machines. Slaves did all of this work by hand.

The pyramids of Egypt are famous archaeological sites. Pharaohs, rulers of vast empires, were buried here with large amounts of furniture, tools, and even food!

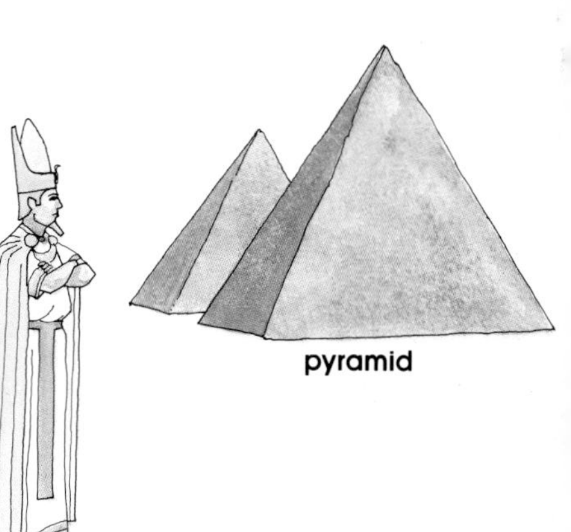

Cliff Palace at Mesa Verde National Park near Cortez, Colorado once housed more than 400 people.

Archaeological sites may be very big. These cliff homes were built more than 900 years ago. Archaeologists think the people left here because of a great drought.

Archaeologist (above) works on a skull at the National Museum in Nairobi, Kenya. Workers (left) uncover the walls of an Aztec temple in Mexico City, Mexico.

Archaeologists go to school for many years and study many subjects. In college, archaeology students learn about ancient cultures. They learn how people from around the world live

Only careful excavation prevented the skeletons (above right) found in the Dickson burial mounds in Illinois and the carving (right) found in an ancient Inca house in Peru from being damaged.

today. Students also learn about subjects such as geology or zoology.

Archaeology students

Archaeologists do much of their work outside.

go on digs. They learn proper excavation techniques. They learn by doing archaeological work and by studying

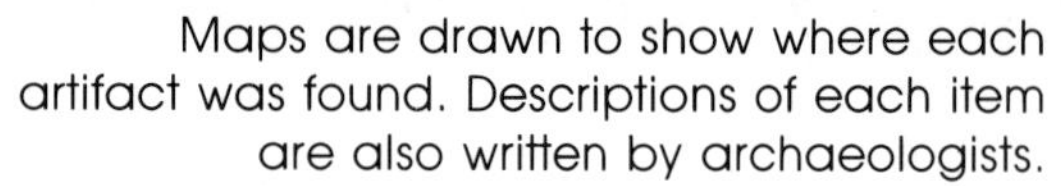

Maps are drawn to show where each artifact was found. Descriptions of each item are also written by archaeologists.

different kinds of artifacts.

To be a professional archaeologist, a student must be a good observer, good excavator, and good writer. Professional archaeologists usually have a Ph.D. degree. This is the highest degree a university can give.

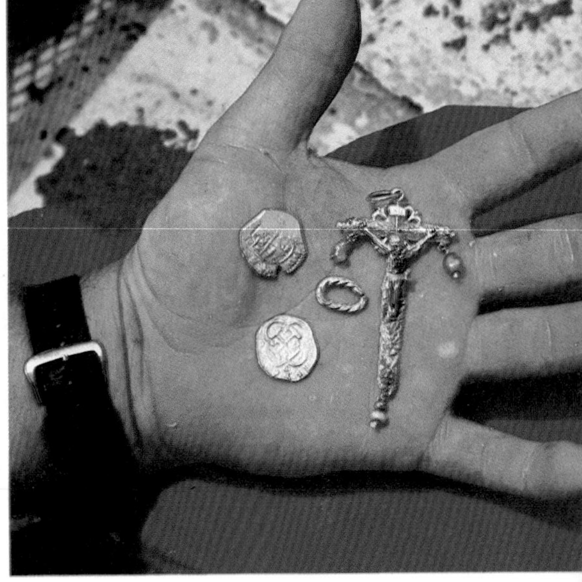

Some archaeologists work underwater. The silver ingots (left) and the gold coins and crucifix (above) were discovered on a sunken ship.

Archaeologists work in universities or museums. From these places, archaeologists do research and write about their finds. Archaeologists

An archaeologist works on an Aztec artifact in a Mexican museum.

who work in a university also teach students to become future archaeologists.

In museums, archaeologists help build exhibits about past civilizations. The

Visitor examines the coffin of King Tut in the Cairo Museum.

museum archaeologist may also be a conservator. He or she specializes in preserving delicate artifacts that are hundreds or even thousands of years old.

Finding the clues and solving the mysteries of the past can be fun. Do you wonder about ancient people? Have you found things and wanted to know what they were or who made them? If you have, you too may want to become an archaeologist!

Opposite page: Archaeologists uncover an Indian skeleton.

CLUES FROM PICTURES ON PAGE 9

1.Q —When was it made?

A—1986

2.Q—From what material was it made?

A—Metal, mainly copper but with small amounts of other metals included

3.Q—What language did the people speak?

A—English

4.Q—Can you find the phrase that is in a second language? What is the language?

A—The phrase is "E Pluribus Unum." It is written in Latin. It means "one out of many" or "one composed of many."

5.Q—Who is the person on the penny?

A—Abraham Lincoln

6.Q—What is the building on the other side of the coin?

A—The Lincoln Memorial in Washington, D.C.

7.Q—In what country was the penny made?

A—The United States of America

8.Q—How is the man wearing his hair?

A—He is wearing fairly short hair and a beard—just like some men wear their hair today.

9.Q—Do the people have a religion?

A—Yes, see the phrase, "In God we trust"?

10.Q—How is the coin used?

A—The coin is used to buy things.

## WORDS YOU SHOULD KNOW

**artifact** (AR • tih • fakt)—something made or shaped by human work

**clue** (KLOO)—something that helps toward solving a problem

**college** (KAH • lij)—a school that offers degrees in a particular field or profession, as law, medicine, agriculture; one of several schools that form a university

**conservator** (kun • SER • vi • tor)—a person who protects or preserves objects

**degree** (dih • GREE)—a title awarded to a student who has completed studies in a particular course

**detective** (dih • TEK • tiv)—a person who investigates and searches out information

**digs** (DIGZ)—places where archaeologists dig to search for ancient artifacts, buildings, cities

**empire** (EM • pyre)—the lands or nations, ruled by an emperor

**excavation** (x • kah • VAY • shun)—pit created by digging

**geology** (gee • AHL • uh • gee)—the science that studies the earth's beginning and structure

**mystery** (MISS • tree)—anything unexplained, unknown, not understood, arousing curiosity

**objects** (AHB • jekts)—material things; anything that can be seen or touched

**observer** (ahb • ZER • ver)—one who sees or watches attentively

**palaces** (PAL • iss • sez)—official residences of royalty, usually large and richly furnished

**pyramids** (PEER • ah • midz)—monuments usually built square at base, with four triangular sides meeting at a top point

**sites** (SYTES)—locations; a land area set apart for a specific use

**technique** (tek • NEEK)—a refined, practiced method used to make or do something

**zoology** (zoo • AHL • ih • gee)—the scientific study of animals

## INDEX



## PHOTO CREDITS

© Reinhard Brucker—9 (left)

© Cameramann International Ltd.—17 (left)

EKM-Nepenthe:
© G.H. Matchneer—15

Gartman Agency:
© Frank Siteman—Cover

© Virginia Grimes—20 (top right)

Journalism Services:
© Mark Gamba—20 (bottom right)

Nawrocki Stock Photo:
© William S. Nawrocki—4, 9 (right), 13 (left)
© Robert B. Pickering—13 (right), 23 (2 photos)

Odyssey Productions:
© Robert Frerck—19 (2 photos), 24 (2 photos)

Root Resources:
© Margaret Crader—18
© Mary A. Root—21
© Loren M. Root—26

Tom Stack & Associates:
© Bob Gossington—6 (top left)
© John Pawloski—6 (bottom left)
© William Patterson—12 (2 photos)
© Ann & Myron Sutton—17 (right)
© Thomas Kitchin—20 (left)
© M. Timothy O'Keefe—25

Valan Photos:
© Kennon Cooke—6 (top right)
© Val & Alan Wilkinson—16 (4 photos), 22 (2 photos)

## ABOUT THE AUTHOR

Robert B. Pickering received his Ph.D. in archaeology and physical anthropology from Northwestern University in 1984. For the last fifteen years, Dr. Pickering has done archaeological research in the American Midwest, Mexico, and on islands in the Pacific Ocean. In addition to research, Dr. Pickering has been a lecturer and teacher of anthropology in universities, professional organizations, and at the Field Museum of natural History. His hobbies include photography and gardening.